THE THRILL IS GONE

YOUR RELATIONSHIP MIGHT BE IN TROUBLE IF...

BY Joe Hobby

ILLUSTRATED BY FRANK CUMMINGS

The Best of Times, Inc.

Pelham, Alabama

Thanks!

Joe Hobby

1

Library of Congress Cataloging in Publication Data

Hobby, Joe
    The Thrill Is Gone
ISBN 1-886049-05-X

Distributed By Southern Publishers Group
1-800-628-0903

Dedication

This book was purchased for _____

because of the following pages:

1. _____

2. _____

3. _____

4. _____

5. _____

If more than 5 pages apply to you, I've taken your photo out of my billfold.

Foreword

I first met Joe Hobby several years ago when he began writing jokes for me. Later, I learned that in addition to being a clever writer, Joe is a talented stand up comedian, a very funny guy! Now he's written a book that's as entertaining as he is.

I enjoyed reading Joe's book and think you will, too.

—Jay Leno

Introduction

You've heard it before. Time and time again—at the office, at the gym, or while your nails are being done. People are discussing their love life. Saying things like, "One day I just walked in and, boom! She told me it was over." Or, "I don't get it. Out of the blue, he tells me he doesn't love me anymore." Hey, I'm sure that this happens, but I think that most of the time, the demise of a relationship is like a coronary. Both have warning signs that point to trouble. In either case, if you ignore the symptoms, you can end up with a damaged heart. About the only difference between the two is that Blue Cross won't cover legal bills.

And some of the symptoms are so obvious. For example, a man who picks up an anniversary present at 7-Eleven can hurt a girl's feelings, especially if she doesn't like Slim Jims. On the other hand, screaming out an ex-boyfriend's name at a crucial moment can bruise the frail male ego—and it's even worse if your current boyfriend happens to walk into the room.

People in questionable relationships shouldn't have to guess, they need to know! That's why I wrote this book.

So, sit back with someone you love, turn the pages, and see if any of the warning signs apply. Maybe you'll be able to tell if your love boat is about to turn into the *Titanic*.

—JH

The only time you wrestle on the sofa is for possession of the remote control.

Your relationship might be in trouble if...

You think a "driver's side airbag" means your spouse is behind the wheel.

Your relationship might be in trouble if...

The PTA meeting and McDonald's is a big night out.

Your relationship might be in trouble if...

You have to drink your spouse pretty.

Your relationship might be in trouble if...

He brings a date home for dinner.

Your relationship might be in trouble if...

Her pin cushion looks like a voodoo doll of you.

Your relationship might be in trouble if...

He puts your fishnet hose in his tackle box.

Your relationship might be in trouble if...

An "Over 1 Million Served" sign shows up in your front yard.

OVER 1 MILLION SERVED

DRIVE·THRU

His best friend is inflatable.

Your relationship might be in trouble if...

She sleeps in sweatpants and ties knots in the drawstring.

Your relationship might be in trouble if...

Your batteries keep mysteriously disappearing
from your flashlight.

Your relationship might be in trouble if...

You've ever used your wedding photos to line the bird cage.

He asks you to "pull his finger"
in front of your mother.

Your relationship might be in trouble if...

He wears a black arm band on your anniversary.

Your relationship might be in trouble if...

She gets a Christmas card from Motel 6.

Your relationship might be in trouble if...

Geraldo rejected you because you were too weird.

Your relationship might be in trouble if...

NOW SHOWING:
THE BIG BANG THEORY
xxxxxxxxx

The PITZ Theater

The only time he takes you to the movies he brings a roll of quarters.

Your relationship might be in trouble if...

You go for more than four weeks without shaving your legs.

Your relationship might be in trouble if...

Any of your arguments have been featured on "Cops".

32

Your relationship might be in trouble if...

You find "The Club" across your bedroom door.

She's ever forced you to take more than 3 tests in *Cosmopolitan* magazine.

Your relationship might be in trouble if...

The only scoring play he cares about is on television.

Your relationship might be in trouble if...

He intentionally leaves the toilet seat up after you go to bed.

Your relationship might be in trouble if...

You discover she's filled out a change of address kit with your name on it.

Your relationship might be in trouble if...

You think someone saying "I got a car for my wife" refers to a good trade.

Your relationship might be in trouble if...

The dog is the only one who humps your leg.

Your relationship might be in trouble if...

He used to look like Prince Charming—
and now he just looks like Prince.

Your relationship might be in trouble if...

You're gone on an overnight trip and she doesn't notice.

Your relationship might be in trouble if...

She keeps a can of mace on the nightstand.

Your relationship might be in trouble if...

She's ever "hit on" your marriage counselor.

Your relationship might be in trouble if...

You've ever been forced to shave your spouse's back.

Your relationship might be in trouble if...

She sleeps with a butcher knife.

He's ever traded his wedding ring for a trolling motor.

Your relationship might be in trouble if...

She smears meat tenderizer on your back
before you swim in the ocean.

Your relationship might be in trouble if...

She puts a "Just say no" bumper sticker on the headboard.

Your relationship might be in trouble if...

He plays poker with the guys on your wedding night.

Your relationship might be in trouble if...

Her gynecologist sees her naked more than you do.

His monthly
1-900 bills are
more than your
house payment.

Your relationship might be in trouble if...

"Bad gas" usually ends up inside of the car
instead of in the tank.

Your relationship might be in trouble if...

He walks past Victoria's Secret to get to Sears.

You catch him watching your exercise video
in slow motion.

Your relationship might be in trouble if...

His idea of a romantic evening is a six pack and a Stallone video.

59

Your relationship might be in trouble if...

You believe abstinence is an effective method of birth control.

JUST SAY...
YECCHH!

Your relationship might be in trouble if...

You catch her putting saltpeter in your orange juice.

Your relationship might be in trouble if...

You've ever had a fight during communion.

Your relationship might be in trouble if...

He comes home with a tatoo of another woman's name.

TONYA

Your relationship might be in trouble if...

He thinks foreplay refers to a group
on a golf course.

Your relationship might be in trouble if...

The last time you saw her strip she was refinishing furniture.

Your relationship might be in trouble if...

You discover she's calling her own vibrating beeper.

Your relationship might be in trouble if...

You both cry at weddings — for entirely different reasons.

Your relationship might be in trouble if...

He takes you to Hooters for your anniversary dinner.

Your relationship might be in trouble if...

He's ever suggested that you "trade out" for that $1,200 transmission job.

WHY, SHORE!

Your relationship might be in trouble if...

He buys more jewelry for himself than he does for you.

Your relationship might be in trouble if...

He can't stay up to watch a late night movie with you, but he has no trouble getting up at 4 a.m. to go fishing.

Your relationship might be in trouble if...

You ask her to play "Post Office" and she gets an assault weapon.

Your relationship might be in trouble if...

The last crabs he brought home didn't come from Long John Silver's.

Your relationship might be in trouble if...

You overhear her say, "Yes, but he's not their father."

Your relationship might be in trouble if...

He leaves you in labor to make a tee off time.

WOULD'YA LOOK AT THE TIME!...

Your relationship might be in trouble if...

He passes gas in a crowd and blames it on you.

Your relationship might be in trouble if...

He recorded over your wedding video with a rerun of Gilligan's Island.

Your relationship might be in trouble if...

You've only recently discovered that your sexy lingerie is several sizes too small.